This notebook Belongs to: